HELD TOGETHER WITH TAPE AND GLUE

poems by

Pamela Hobart Carter

Finishing Line Press
Georgetown, Kentucky

HELD TOGETHER WITH TAPE AND GLUE

Copyright © 2021 by Pamela Hobart Carter
ISBN 978-1-64662-571-0 First Edition
All rights reserved under International and Pan-American Copyright Conventions. No part of this book may be reproduced in any manner whatsoever without written permission from the publisher, except in the case of brief quotations embodied in critical articles and reviews.

ACKNOWLEDGMENTS

Thank you to *The Pangolin Review* in which COMMONPLACE EPIPHANIES appeared.

EVERYDAY LIKE A FOREST and EXPRESSION are erasures from *Auguste Rodin* by Rainer Maria Rilke, translated by Daniel Slager. Lines in italics are quotations.

SEEKING SELF-IMPROVEMENT and ANOTHER FACTOR OF SNOW are erasures from *Self-Editing for Fiction Writers* by Renni Browne and Dave King.

Publisher: Leah Huete de Maines
Editor: Christen Kincaid
Cover Art: Pamela Hobart Carter using a photograph by Robert M L Raynard
Author Photo: Omar Willey, https://creativecommons.org/licenses/by/4.0/
Cover Design: Elizabeth Maines McCleavy

Order online: www.finishinglinepress.com
       also available on amazon.com

Author inquiries and mail orders:
Finishing Line Press
PO Box 1626
Georgetown, Kentucky 40324
USA

Table of Contents

Flight Over a Quiet Square 1

Everyday like a Forest 2

Occasion 3

Expression 4

Notice 5

Bed 6

Seeking Self-Improvement 7

Convalescence 8

Another Factor of Snow 9

On the Word 10

About Living 12

Foresee the Cloudhorse 13

Firsthand 14

How To Go at It 15

Beyond the Human Range 16

Relined 17

Commonplace Epiphanies 18

FLIGHT OVER A QUIET SQUARE

inspired by a photograph by Robert M L Raynard

When a bird flies toward you
and you raise your lens,
you can't be sure the solar angle
or the contrast between its white plumage
and the shaded verticals of formal colonnades
and fancy fenestration behind it
will show to the advantage you imagine. You frame
strong sun painting feathers bright
through the gull's fanned tail
and wing edge, the flying form
at an active banking angle
about to alight on pale gray pavers,
discretely delineated foreground.
We dream of flight. Of riding sky.
Of letting a wind
hold us aloft. Landing as easily here
as on a rooftop.

EVERYDAY LIKE A FOREST

> "*Rodin was not presumptuous enough to create trees.*"
> from *Auguste Rodin* by Rainer Maria Rilke,
> translated by Daniel Slager

Every day like a forest
never losing an hour,
we remember how small
human hands are,
how little a nation,
life a passing.

    Years know nothing.

Childhood still belongs
to truth, is present
and alive, a narrative
with burdens.

    It seemed more important to carve
    in wood with a dull knife
    luminous objects, nameless.
    Even sparrows and turtles
    (at least one of every kind) transformed
    into what they were now without memory
    of another existence. Nearby bells
    adapted vitality, fervent
    and impetuous.

    All humble gestures,
    no less beautiful than this body
    adorned with light, infused with twilight,
    like the petal carried
    endlessly.

    One must never hurry.

OCCASION

On occasion the threat is real and you have seen it.
Nerve endings are many and astute.

Perhaps you understand? Tragedies
spool from every source. Not the sight of blood,

but its scent and taste draw the shark.
As obediently undertaken as an assignment,

as a suspension of ordinary time, carry your blaze
always to undo acts of evil men.

Share an unworldly weight of sunrays
in these woods. Follow the unfamiliar drums

when the maple turns. See
the pale gibbous glow. Most miss

the mid-morning moon, the whole ocean
of dreamed life.

EXPRESSION

With an expression of tenderness
a silent night emanates. One hardly dares
ascribe meaning. Thoughts pass,
not forgotten. Radiance comes
from contact, another rendering
of union, bodies touching at
many places. More points
of contact like chemicals
of great affinity. A new whole
moving depths of memory
on and on beyond.

Bodies came into their own, just.
There were no denials or lies.
They were honest and great,
no longer overpowered.

Glory comes like a smile,
like storms. Power is won,
strangely linked together—
reflection and spontaneity. Bodies
clinging, bodies listen like faces.
Beings together with force and majesty
and all strength, the strength of action,
complete and perfectly defined.

Air wafts around them as it does around rocks.
Sky rises with them.

NOTICE

All has been harrowed and harrowing from tears over-spilling levees.

Waiting to understand, to hum, you hunt for the methods.

Patterns are easier to see from the sky.

Those beans you found, you planted and believed magical.

No catastrophe interrupts.

Notice good things—the ocean, how bees visit all blooms not only those sown by hands.

Wait for the sweet heft of jasmine.

It happens to you.

Freshness comes, a cornucopia of exuberance.

BED

say and do
        the mind
to smooth.
        make ready
for the day.
        tug the corner
to match
        the corner
of the other
        side. round
the end. tug
        in passing
striking
        symmetry.
tug so upon
        the other
side. hand
        as iron
press. press
        sheet over
hem in pas
        sing. smooth
as. smooth
        the mind.
done said
        done. and day
is readymade.

SEEKING SELF-IMPROVEMENT

Contrary to popular wisdom,
a book will cure your planet in this century.

As a result, your flair seems more natural, gives a little snap.

Answer the unspoken. Talk, hedge, disagree.
Notice the subtle authenticity in line.

An exact transcription is artifice that mimics
normal life. Be alert for any mistake.
It may be an improvement.

CONVALESCENCE

A whole century passes
in a single night.
Embrace darkness, darling.

Brain struggling during sleep
sweeps, bends, swoops trees aside.
Trumpets blare announcement:

fair news foams
on the sand. Everything happens
in five minutes—scenes undergo

large and rapid changes. The optimist scans
the scrub for helpful shadows.
There is a chance we emerge convalesced.

ANOTHER FACTOR OF SNOW

Another factor that controls a New England snowstorm
is a little girl delighting in her first winter.

One of the most vital descriptions conveys texture
so subtle nearly all color shifts to the distance.

Time, somewhat compressed, is tinged
with edginess. If the world is your powerful snowfall,

proportion problems arise while you sleep.
Most may be avoided. The trick is telling

the difference between what really comes
and what is uncomfortable. Be prepared

for a shrewd detective in a village
of old biddies, a chance meeting, like so many.

ON THE WORD

Here we are. On the page. On the word.
On the dot or the hook or the serif.

Here we are. In the big city. In this house.
In this room or the kitchen. Here lies truth.

Truth lies, here on the sofa, with us,
where our feet are up, stocking-footed,

shoes tidily stowed in the closet
when we came in from clearing dead leaves

from the hollyhocks. This morning, as yesterday,
and the hundreds of days before, we made our beds,

raised our blinds, breakfasted, despite the churn
in our guts forecasting world's end.

That day has not come. We lied in saying, here we are.
We are at a distance. We must shout until we arrive,

until allowed to arrive, or led to the small room
where we die. In the days to come we will tend our gardens,

some of which are tiny pots on a windowsill.
Like old fashioned desk blotters turning ink drops

into soft-edged disks, we'll drink in sunshine.
Soon darkness will enshroud us.

We are, throughout, so typically ourselves, frantic
about tumbling through rabbit holes, although we'd love to land

in a magic place. Gleeful at the tree turning pink, the sky
going blue. Thrilled by a phrase in a book.

We even jot it down to remember. The scaffold always rattles.
Every tower crumbles. We cry and laugh about details, generalities.

How did we get so good at calendars and clocks,
still ignorant of true passage?

ABOUT LIVING

"Where do you come from?" ask directly of realms dreamed.

Fathom they come from your own mind.

Record discoveries of things swimming inside.

Fashion translations into the open, your body as conveyance.

Also, climb trees, explore old barns—places forbidden, exiles, and homelands.

FORESEE THE CLOUDHORSE

Don't we find what we foresee?

Is it a sort of universal law,
particles spelling the message
available only as wavelengths
of imagination that daily pass,
so as to return us
to a state of wonder?

To set our dreams upon?

To set our dreams upon,
like a song now,
a cloudhorse gallops
across a blue meadow.

FIRSTHAND

Reuse Monet's haystacks
and meadows, bogs
and rivers. Include ordinary water,
mist, and ice. Associate everything—
thorns may point to red, to circulation,
a royal universe.

Clasp and hold—floating—
the intricate craft
of the heart. Bask calloused fingers
in the tributaries. Grow, out of facts
habitually forgotten, a family—
brightly colored—of women
preparing to speak.

HOW TO GO AT IT

With fertile velocity, no fake scraping or bowing.

A meticulous approach, because key moments

are both fragile

and profound, swift to quash

with a stumble.

Through the gate to this garden, we find thistles

and bird vetch, as well as roses.

Notice how bees visit all blooms,

not only those sown by hands.

Inhale this sweetness, this tang.

BEYOND THE HUMAN RANGE

Ospreys perceive a range beyond our human spectrum

    into ultraviolet,
        hues incomprehensible,

available only as wavelengths of imagination.

Are we too big to catch the acute hunter's scope

    as we (un-furred
        and in-delicious),

play hopscotch across sunny sidewalks and empty lots?

Our cones do celebrate the swishing tints of blue and tangerine

    that surround us
        and supply our inner vision.

We paint what we suppose ospreys survey and never miss what we cannot see.

RELINED

Look at the world
as if for the first time

Beside us
rivers
A sense of passage

to carry your self
into its next version

Or I am wrong
All lines dissolve
long before a few traditions

quietly drift
to a shadowy corner

Birds sing more complex melodies
Air brings salt
to already salty face

You brought
into this singular nebulous embrace

patience
to carry your self
into its next version

When will we fly
Not by chance

you sing with me
to carry your self
into its next version

COMMONPLACE EPIPHANIES

While you nap
      the world as you know it pulses
(not as a heart but)

            in the way of celestial bodies
jingling according to private sheet music

It seems when you wake
          a whole new sphere chimes around you

You recognize this home
          It isn't a mirage or a prior century
      No minstrel sings below your castle wall

          You consider that the changes may be your own

            something interior
    and of nearly-invisible dimension

        or perhaps you and the earth
          mutated synchronously

None of your friends notice how altered you are since last reckoning

While sleeping you lived in a forlorn kingdom
   of velvet and silver and lost jewels

      A troubadour did serenade you

   or was an owl asking
          if it were alone

Most of us doubt the individual's power to metamorphose
      and yet this globe
          and you and I
   have been at least seven mortals apiece
       since Monday noon

After earning two degrees in geology (Bryn Mawr College and Indiana University), **Pamela Hobart Carter** became a teacher and taught for more than thirty years. Her plays have been read and produced in Montreal (where she grew up), Seattle (where she lives), and Fort Worth (where she has only visited). Her poetry has appeared in *Pif*, *The Seattle Star*, and *Barrow Street*, among others.

www.ingramcontent.com/pod-product-compliance
Lightning Source LLC
LaVergne TN
LVHW041525070426
835507LV00013B/1829